29

D1171054

Steve Jobs
Computer Genius of Apple

INTERNET BIOGRAPHIES

BILL GATES
Software Genius of Microsoft
0-7660-1969-1

LARRY ELLISON
Database Genius of Oracle
0-7660-1974-8

ESTHER DYSON
Internet Visionary
0-7660-1973-X

STEVE CASE
Internet Genius of America Online
0-7660-1971-3

JEFF BEZOS
Business Genius of Amazon.com
0-7660-1972-1

STEVE JOBS
Computer Genius of Apple
0-7660-1970-5

INTERNET BIOGRAPHIES

Steve Jobs
Computer Genius of Apple

by Virginia Brackett

Enslow Publishers, Inc.

40 Industrial Road   PO Box 38
Box 398   Aldershot
Berkeley Heights, NJ 07922   Hants GU12 6BP
USA   UK

http://www.enslow.com

PRODUCED BY:
Chestnut Productions
Russell, Massachusetts

Editor and Picture Researcher: *Mary E. Hull*
Design and Production: *Lisa Hochstein*

Library of Congress Cataloging-in-Publication Data

Brackett, Virginia.
  Steve Jobs : computer genius of Apple / by Virginia Brackett.
     p. cm. — (Internet biographies)
Summary: A biography of the founder of Apple Computer company and owner of Pixar, the computer animation company that developed the movie "Toy Story."
  ISBN 0-7660-1970-5
  1. Jobs, Steven, 1955—Juvenile literature. 2. Computer engineers—United States—Biography—Juvenile literature. 3. Apple Computer, Inc.—History—Juvenile literature. [1. Jobs, Steven, 1955- 2. Computer engineers 3. Businesspeople. 4. Computer industry. 5. Apple Computer, Inc. 6. Pixar (Firm) 7. Computer animation.] I. Title. II. Series.
QA76.2.J63B73 2003
621.39'092—dc21

                           2002153287

Printed in the United States of America

10 9 8 7 6 5 4 3 2 1

To Our Readers:
We have done our best to make sure all Internet addresses in this book were active and appropriate when we went to press. However, the author and the publisher have no control over and assume no liability for the material available on those Internet sites or on other Web sites they may link to. Any comments or suggestions can be sent by e-mail to comments@enslow.com or to the address on the back cover.

Illustration Credits: Associated Press/Wide World Photos, pp. 2, 9, 18, 20, 25, 27, 28, 30, 36, 41; Corbis, pp. 12, Getty Images, p. 6.

Cover Illustration: Associated Press/Wide World Photos

Opposite Title Page: *Steve Jobs announced the company's plans to open Apple retail stores around the country in 2001. Previously Apple had relied on resellers and its Web site to sell computers.*

CONTENTS

With the success of the movie Toy Story, *Steve Jobs and the Pixar animation studio gained recognition.* Toy Story *was so popular it inspired a sequel,* Toy Story 2.

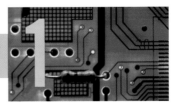

Victory

On November 22, 1995, guests poured into a building to see *Toy Story,* the first full-length movie created entirely with computer animation. A company called Pixar developed the animation. When the movie ended, the guests clapped loudly. They used words like "genius" to describe this new type of film. It was the same word often used to describe Pixar's owner, Steve Jobs.

Most people did not know that Steve Jobs had helped to develop *Toy Story.* They knew him as the founder of Apple Computer, the company that introduced the personal computer to the world. Apple's user-friendly computers had revolutionized the computer industry. They had changed the way people felt about computers. Now, nearly twenty years after Jobs first entered public life, he was returning to the winner's circle with Pixar. *Toy Story* proved to be a huge success, earning $29 million during its opening weekend.

Those who knew Steve Jobs well were not surprised. Pixar was one more success out of many for Jobs. When Jobs bought Pixar in 1986, it had not yet produced a film. Nevertheless, Jobs thought the animation studio had promise. He bought it from its owner, *Star Wars* movie director George Lucas, for $10 million.

When Jobs bought Pixar, it was a small company that employed forty-four people. Over the next two years, Jobs saw his company grow and develop other films. In 1988, the Pixar film *Tin Toy* won an Academy Award. Soon Pixar began producing award-winning commercials. Then it began to work with the Walt Disney studio in making commercials and films. While Jobs did not actually work on the movies, he supported the work. He had the vision to see how important Pixar's work would be.

Computer animation was a new concept. Previously, artists had created animated, or moving, images by hand. They drew one scene at a time on paper or plastic, and a camera filmed the scenes in separate frames. Each frame quickly followed another. This made the audience see "moving" images. With computer animation, however, the computer controlled the art and the movement. This enabled filmmakers to create special effects never before possible. But developing this kind of animation was costly and time consuming. For *Toy Story,* the studio spent between three and twenty-four hours on each

This is a frame from the Disney/Pixar film A Bug's Life. *Pixar developed special computer animation techniques that helped make its characters come alive.*

frame. More than 100,000 frames were required. Luckily, the studio used many computers. The project would have taken one computer thirty-eight years to complete!

Nearly ten years after Jobs purchased Pixar, he could finally celebrate with the success of *Toy Story.* He had introduced the world to another successful "first." After *Toy Story,* Jobs took another bold step. He decided to sell shares of stock in Pixar to the public. That meant that anyone could buy a piece of Pixar. The money from the sale of stock would help support Pixar and pay for research into new technology. Jobs boldly planned Pixar's first stock sale for November 29, 1995, just one week after the public fell in love with *Toy Story.*

PIXAR AND COMPUTER ANIMATION

As of 2002, Steve Jobs was chairman and chief executive officer (CEO) of Pixar. The Academy Award winning company has produced popular feature films like *Toy Story, Toy Story 2, A Bug's Life,* and *Monsters, Inc.* Pixar developed its own software, or computer instructions, to create its high-quality computer animation.

It takes many steps to turn a story idea into an animated film. First, artists create storyboards, or sketches, of the movie's scenes. They create different looks for when a character is happy or angry or sad. They also create backgrounds and props for the different scenes in the story. Characters, scenes, and props can then be sculpted by hand and scanned-in three-dimensionally into a computer. They can also be modeled in 3-D directly in the computer. Characters are then given "avars," or hinges, which animators use to make them move. The face of a character may have as many as one hundred avars. This is so it can be moved many different ways. To create motion, animators act like puppeteers, making the characters move with computer controls. Each scene is recorded in the computer. The computer data is then rendered, or translated, into film. Each frame of the movie takes about six hours to render, even though it only lasts for a fraction of a second. Professional actors record voices for all the characters by reading from a script. The movie is then set to music and given sound effects and special effects. Throughout the process, a lot of editing and adjusting takes place. The films require a lot of polishing before they are ready to be shown.

To learn more about the computer animation process and the Pixar company, check out their Web site at http://www.pixar.com

On the morning of the sale, Jobs made a dramatic entrance. He arrived at the investment bank just before the action began. Pixar's financial officer wanted to set the price at $15 per share of stock. Jobs wanted to take a bigger risk. He had always believed in following his dreams. He set the price at $22 per share. Once again, Steve Jobs proved himself a winner. In the first thirty minutes, the stock price shot up to $49. Within an hour, Steve Jobs's worth skyrocketed to almost $1.5 billion. His faith in Pixar had paid off. Pixar had faced many failures, but Steve Jobs was not afraid of failure. As one Pixar employee said, "he kept writing the checks."[1] That showed that he believed in his company.

Jobs had once again captured the public's attention. He offered the world a promise. It could look to Steve Jobs and computers for a better future.

When Steve Jobs was born, computers still used thousands of vacuum tubes and could weigh as much as thirty tons. This computer, first introduced in 1946, was called ENIAC.

A Young Man with a Vision

Steve Jobs was born Steve Paulis on February 24, 1955. Paul and Clara Jobs adopted him as an infant. He grew up in Mountain View, California, south of San Francisco. Clara and Paul also adopted a daughter, Patti. Paul Jobs was a high school dropout. He worked at different jobs, running machines. Clara Jobs helped support the family. She had a part-time job as a payroll clerk, and she sometimes babysat for other children. The extra money helped to pay for things like swimming lessons for Steve and Patti.

In junior high school, Steve did not get along with his classmates. He liked to be by himself. He was bright and creative, but he had a hard time at school. Steve was enrolled in a program for gifted students. He was so smart, his teachers suggested that he skip a grade. Still, he did not have many friends. The other children considered him different and strange. But even though other kids made fun of him, Steve had faith in himself.

When he was in the seventh grade, Steve's parents moved the family to Los Altos, California. Around this time, Steve began to work with his father on machinery. He learned a lot about how things were put together. He used his imagination to invent machines his father had never seen. At age thirteen, he built a crude calculator. He could choose numbers on a keypad that allowed him to work math problems. Steve placed first in a science fair with his invention.

Steve entered Homestead High School in Los Altos as a freshman. His electronics teacher said Steve "always had a different way of seeing things."[1] For one electronics project, Steve needed special parts. He did not order them through a store. In an unusual move, Steve called Bill Hewlett, the co-founder of the Hewlett-Packard computer company. Most teens would have been afraid to talk with such an important person. But Steve Jobs was not like most teens. Hewlett admired Steve's initiative, and he sent him a frequency counter. The frequency counter measured the frequency of electricity. It counted how many times per second an electrical current was turned on and off. This focus on timing was crucial to understanding how computers worked.

When Steve Jobs was thirteen he met his future business partner, Steve Wozniak. Steve, or "Woz," as he was called, was eighteen. A college dropout, he worked at Hewlett-Packard. Steve had also begun to work at Hewlett-Packard during summers. He attended lectures the company held. Woz could see that Steve was no ordinary teenager. He decided to join Steve in working on electronics projects.

After graduating from high school, Jobs went to Reed College in Oregon. Once again, he took an unusual approach. He never enrolled in the college. Instead, Jobs talked to the dean in charge of housing. Steve convinced the dean to let him live in a dorm for free. He took classes not to receive a grade, but just to learn. The classes, however, did not satisfy Steve. He dropped out after one semester.

Although no longer attending classes, Steve hung around Reed College. He experimented with unusual

HOW COMPUTERS COMPUTE

Computers use units of measure based on the binary numbering system. The binary numbering system uses only two digits: zero and one. Human beings use the decimal system. It uses the numbers zero, one, two, three, four, five, six, seven, eight, and nine. Although "kilo" stands for a thousand, a kilobyte is not equal to 1,000 bytes. It's equal to 1,024 bytes. Computers deal with some very large numbers. Here's one way to keep up with it all:

8 bits = 1 byte

1,024 bytes = 1 kilobyte (K)

1,024 K = 1 megabyte (MB)

1,024 MB = 1 gigabyte (GB)

diets. He once drank so much carrot juice his skin turned orange. One friend feared that Steve had an eating disorder. Later Jobs admitted that he dealt with life at this time "in my typical nutso way."[2]

For several years, Jobs drifted. He searched for answers to questions about his life. Then he took a job designing video games for a company called Atari. When that did not satisfy him, he took a trip. He traveled to India with a friend, hoping to find spiritual direction. Although he enjoyed the different culture, he was not satisfied. He decided to return to the United States.

Jobs reunited with his old friend Steve Wozniak in Palo Alto, California. He joined Woz's electronics club. The club was made up of engineers and other people who enjoyed talking about computers as a hobby. At last, Jobs found others who shared his interest in computers.

Jobs wanted to develop and sell gadgets based on Woz's ideas. Woz loved electronics, but he had no interest in business. So the two teamed up and put together a crude computer. It had a simple central processing unit (CPU) that ran the computer. The CPU cost twenty-five dollars. The machine used a tiny bit of material called a computer chip. The chip contained a clock and could perform math calculations. Unfortunately, the computer could not remember information. It did not even have a keyboard. But it could calculate reliably.

Jobs named their invention "Apple." He invited others to join him and Woz in forming a company. Later, the group adopted a simple logo—an apple. The apple had layers of color and one bite taken from it. The bite acted as wordplay on the computer term, "byte." A byte is a group of eight computer "bits." A bit is the smallest unit of information that a computer can handle.

Jobs and Woz dreamed of a computer made for non-experts. They imagined people using this kind of computer in their homes. Today many people have computers at home, but at that time, only businesses used computers. Business computers were large and bulky, and the average person did not know how to use one. Computers had not yet been designed for personal use. The two Steves set out to change all that.

Their first step was to design this new kind of machine. It had to be something that people with no special training could use. The second step was to build it. Woz could handle both of those steps, with some help from Jobs. The third step was to sell this new idea to the world. This step fell to Jobs alone. But Jobs was no ordinary salesman. He sometimes made visits to sellers while barefoot. From the very beginning, he made it clear that Apple was going to be a different kind of computer company.

The two Steves designed the first Apple personal computer in Jobs's bedroom. They built it in his

Steve Wozniak shows off the Apple IIg computer, the first Apple that used a color monitor. Woz and Jobs were childhood friends who enjoyed tinkering with electronics.

garage. Only later would they realize the importance of their creation. It would literally change the world. Soon everyone would know the story of the young men and their amazing machine.

Jobs showed the first machine they created to a local seller who ordered twenty-five of them. Jobs and Woz celebrated, but they knew they needed money to finance their vision. Woz sold his prized Hewlett-Packard calculator, and Jobs sold his Volkswagen bus. These were their favorite things, but their dream was worth the sacrifice. The sales raised $1300.

Local dealers agreed to sell Jobs and Woz electronics parts on credit. The Steves promised to pay them back later. In this way, they were able to produce the first Apple Computers. Unlike other computers, the Apple I came with software, instructions that told the computer what to do.

The Apple I Computer retailed for $666 in 1976. It was the first computer with a built-in reading memory, and it could load information from an outside source. People who enjoyed electronics as a hobby were the perfect customers for the Apple I. In its first year in business, Apple Computer earned $774,000. Jobs used that money to pay expenses and loans. He also bought more materials. Apple was on its way to success.

Jobs convinced Woz to quit his job at Hewlett-Packard and become Apple's vice president of research and development. Wozniak and Jobs, the two outsiders, had not simply founded a company. They had opened new doors to knowledge and creativity. Their personal computers would change the world.

Steve Jobs, above, and Steve Wozniak made their own computer and launched the Apple Company in 1976. One of their earliest models was the Apple II of 1977.

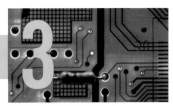

Welcome to the World of Apple

I n 1977, Apple Computer produced the Apple II. The Apple II had something no other small computer had at that time: a color monitor. The color monitor was Jobs's idea. He had another idea to make the computer popular. He urged anyone who designed software to write Apple II programs, or instructions. This allowed Apple users to feel like they were a part of Apple. Eventually 16,000 different programs appeared for the Apple II. Unlike other companies, Apple did not guard its software. Those who designed programs could share them with others. Jobs wanted everyone to be part of his revolution. The public could not get enough of the two Steves and their creation. Apple's personal computers and software had captured the public's attention and its loyalty.

Jobs's success grew with his design of the sleek Apple II. It was one of the first computers enclosed in a plastic case. The case was a handsome beige color.

Users could also add attachments, such as game paddles, to the Apple II.

Apple was so successful that soon other computer makers wanted to get into the personal computer business. One of these makers was a huge company called International Business Machines (IBM). Jobs knew that he needed help to compete against such a giant company. He asked several people to join Apple to support its success. A former Intel marketing manager, Mike Markkula, became the company's first president. Markkula was able to borrow hundreds of thousands of dollars. With this money, Jobs could make his new ideas a reality.

During this time Jobs's girlfriend, Chris-Ann, became pregnant. He and Chris-Ann had dated since high school. Chris-Ann gave birth to a daughter, Lisa, in 1978. Chris-Ann insisted that Jobs take a blood test to determine whether he was Lisa's father. The blood test showed a 94.4 percent chance that he had fathered Lisa. Chris-Ann asked him to pay a one-time settlement of $20,000. Apple's Board of Directors urged Jobs to do so. But he would not pay Chris-Ann the money he could by now afford.

Jobs was known as a moody genius. He could be blunt, outspoken, and sometimes hard to deal with. He had a tendency to ignore or reject the ideas of others. Those who knew him best learned to present their weakest ideas first. They offered their best ideas later, when Jobs might accept them.

Jobs did not choose to live a "normal" life. While he owned a nice house, it had no furniture. He was the millionaire who slept on a mattress on the floor. By now, people had come to expect the unexpected from Jobs.

Jobs believed in doing things differently. This affected the way Apple evolved as a company. Jobs did not want Apple to be like corporate America. He did not want Apple employees to behave like regular nine to five workers. He wanted his workers to be excited about what they were doing. So Jobs hired bright, eccentric engineers. Unlike other companies, Apple did not have a dress code. Its employees did not have to wear suits or ties; they could dress as they pleased. Some observers thought Apple employees were undisciplined. Jobs's critics said the same thing about him. But Jobs believed that Apple's success depended on its imagination.

Apple continued to uphold its reputation as a leader in the computer industry. In 1978 it offered a disk drive designed by Steve Wozniak. Woz's drive wowed the world. Previously, computer software had

---

STEVE JOBS'S NET WORTH

In 1978, Steve Jobs had a worth of $1,000,000.

In 1979, Steve Jobs had a worth of $10,000,000.

In 1980, Steve Jobs had a worth of $100,000,000.

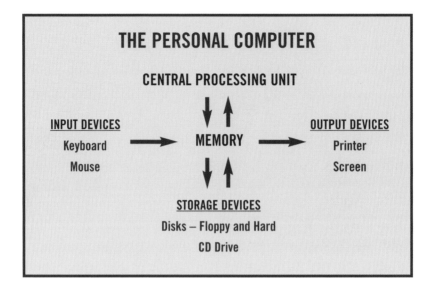

run on a noisy cassette tape player. Woz's disk drive replaced that tape player. With the new drive came an eight-inch square "floppy" plastic disk. The disk contained the information needed to run the computer. Woz's drive design proved extremely popular.

Jobs made sure Apple continued to come up with newer and better innovations. In 1979, Apple created a special program called a spreadsheet. It allowed home users to perform math calculations. Now users did not have to be experts to set up home budgets. Apple's software could help anyone pay their bills and plan their savings.

In 1980, three crucial events occurred in Jobs's life. First, Jobs and the Apple Board decided to sell stock in the company. On the opening day of sales, Apple's stock price rose. It went from $22 to $29 per share. Second, Jobs agreed to recognize Lisa as his

Thousands of Macintosh computers sit on a double-decker manufacturing line at a factory in Fremont, California, in March 1984. The Macintosh was a huge success for Apple.

daughter. He began paying $385 a month in child support to Chris-Ann. Third, Jobs discovered the identity of his birth family.

Jobs's birth mother, Joanne Simpson, was a speech therapist. His father was a political science professor. Jobs had been born before his parents were married. They had made the difficult decision to offer him for adoption. Later they married and had a daughter, Mona Simpson. Mona was a successful author. She and Jobs became good friends.

While Jobs's personal life improved, he experienced setbacks at work. The Apple III computer that Jobs designed in 1981 was a failure. There was a flaw in the early models, and Apple had to recall thousands of computers. And there was another problem.

None of Apple's three computers shared an operating system, which is the software that allows a computer to operate. As a result, they could not share software. Users could not move programs from one Apple computer to another. Even the most devoted Apple fans were unhappy about this.

In 1982 Jobs forged ahead with a another new computer. He named it the "Lisa," after his daughter. The Lisa was the first computer to have a mouse. The mouse was a device that allowed users to easily control the movement of the pointer on the computer screen. Today most computers have a mouse, but back then it was a revolutionary idea. The Lisa was an easy to operate, user-friendly computer. But at $10,000, it was priced too high and did not sell.

Jobs had to deal with these failed products. He also faced more competition in the personal computer field. A company called Microsoft, co-founded by Bill Gates, was just getting started. IBM released its first personal computer in 1981 to great success. By 1983, IBM personal computer sales surpassed those of Apple.

Jobs said, "It would be easy for us to come out with an IBM look-alike product, and put the Apple logo on it . . . but we think that would be the wrong thing to do."[1] Instead, Jobs gave his employees the freedom to create.

In 1984, Apple introduced the Macintosh computer, a machine that offered stunning developments.

Steve Jobs shows off his 1984 creation: the Macintosh. Designed to challenge IBM's personal computer, the Macintosh was the first computer with a graphic interface. It cost $2,495 when it debuted in 1984.

Almost anyone could operate the Macintosh because it had a graphic user interface. With a graphic interface, the computer user does not have to type specific commands into the system. Instead, they can click on pictures and symbols on the screen to ask the computer to perform functions. The Macintosh was the most user-friendly computer available. It did not have the power of IBM's personal computer, but Jobs did not want to compete with IBM in power or strength. He wanted to compete in user-friendliness and creativity. In those areas, the Macintosh easily beat the competition.

The first ad for the new Macintosh aired during the 1984 Super Bowl Game. Jobs wanted to play off

Apple Computer held its first Macworld Conference and Exposition in 1984. Since then, Macworld has become the largest and most popular annual computer convention.

the name of George Orwell's famous novel, *1984.* In that novel, a government nicknamed "Big Brother" tries to take over its citizens' lives. It does not allow for differences. Everyone must dress, think, and act alike. Creativity is discouraged.

In the Macintosh ad, stormtroopers chased a female athlete. She raced past glassy-eyed workers who looked like clones. They were watching the face of Big Brother talk to them from a movie screen. The athlete astounded them by hurling a hammer into the screen, shattering Big Brother. Then a calm voice spoke. It assured viewers that 1984 would not be like *1984,* due to the presence of the Macintosh.

The ad made a huge impression and won awards. Magazines and newspapers asked, "What were you doing when the *1984* commercial ran?"[3] The Macintosh, or "Mac," came to stand for rebellion against the norm.

The Macintosh was both popular and profitable. To celebrate his new machine, Jobs invited Mac users to attend a "Macworld Conference and Exposition" in 1984. Apple users were fiercely loyal to Jobs's company. At Macworld, they exchanged information and ideas. They "test drove" new Mac products. Jobs also asked the visitors' opinions about the Mac. Macworld was such a success it became an annual event. At each Macworld, the public learned of Apple's new products. Afterwards, the value of Apple stock usually increased.

In 1985, Apple sold 400,000 Macintoshes. Apple's success prompted Jobs to give back. He donated Macs to schools through a program he founded called The Kids Can't Wait. Soon, many schools were using Macintosh computers. Jobs also gave Macintoshes to famous people like Beatle John Lennon's wife, Yoko Ono; rock musician Mick Jagger; and artist Andy Warhol. With the success of the Macintosh, Jobs enjoyed his growing fame and the growing reputation of Apple.

Steve Jobs left Apple in 1985 and founded a new computer company called NeXT, which made computers and software for use in education.

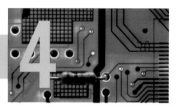

NeXT

Despite the success of the Macintosh, Apple still faced stiff competition in the personal computer field. In 1985, Microsoft introduced its "Windows" software. Like the Macintosh software, it offered a graphic interface that attracted new users. Some people claimed that Microsoft had stolen Apple's technology.

Jobs knew that Apple needed help to succeed against its competitors, so he hired John Sculley, a former Pepsi Cola executive, to be Apple's new president. Jobs had to persuade Sculley to make the move. He told Sculley that at Pepsi, he would only be "selling a lot more sugar water to kids."[1] But if Sculley came to Apple, Jobs told him, he could "change the world."[2] Jobs's argument worked; Sculley moved to Apple.

Before long, however, Sculley turned against Jobs. He did not like the outlaw impression that Jobs had created for Apple. He believed Apple could make more money if its workers followed stricter rules.

Sculley made changes that offended many Apple employees, including Steve Wozniak. Woz had never worked at the company for the sake of money and profits. In 1985, he decided to leave. Onlookers watched his departure with dismay. Woz's engineering ideas had been the heart of Apple.

Jobs stubbornly pursued his vision of Apple as a different kind of company. The Board of Directors, however, did not approve. Nor did they like the fact that he spent most of his energies on the Macintosh. They wanted him to promote additional products.

Jobs's difficult personality made Sculley push hard for his dismissal. He said, "We could run a lot better with Steve out of operations."[3] No one came to Jobs for help or ideas any longer. He compared his disappointment to taking a hard blow to his stomach. He knew, at age thirty, that he needed to leave Apple.

Jobs sold $20 million of his Apple stock and considered his future. He saved the money for a new project, but he had no inspiration. Searching for clues as to what he should do, he biked along the California beach. He toured Paris and parts of Italy. Finally he got an idea after talking with Paul Berg, a Nobel Prize-winning professor at Berkeley University in California. Berg complained of problems with his work, and Jobs asked whether he had tried a computer for help. Berg replied that no computer could do what he needed.

This inspired Jobs to create computers and software for use in colleges and schools. He had already founded several education programs. He considered these programs to be some of the most important work he had ever done. Jobs decided his new focus would be computers and education.

On September 12, 1985, Jobs announced that he was leaving Apple. He told Apple's Board of Directors that he was going to design a computer for use in education. He promised the Board that his new company would not compete with Apple. Jobs said he was taking five Apple employees with him to start his new company. When Sculley found out who was leaving to work with Jobs, he was furious. All five were excellent employees who knew Apple inside and out.

Jobs called his new company NeXT. The beginning of NeXT differed greatly from that of Apple.

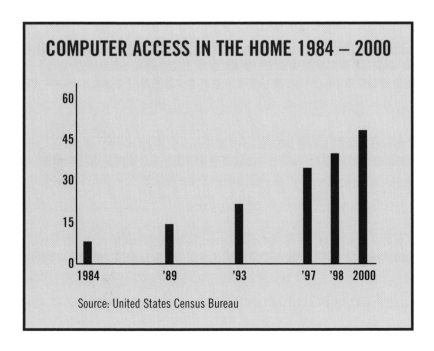

COMPUTER ACCESS IN THE HOME 1984 – 2000

Source: United States Census Bureau

Instead of a garage, NeXT was born in a mansion. The once thrifty Jobs now spent huge amounts of money. Developing the NeXT logo alone cost $100,000. Part of Jobs's inspiration came from his anger at Apple president John Sculley. He made it clear that he wanted revenge on Sculley and Apple. He told one reporter, "Sculley wouldn't know a new product if it hit him on the head."[4]

Jobs found the hiring process at NeXT challenging. He still had a reputation for being hard to work with. In many cases, it was deserved. In one instance, Jobs insulted an accountant who was interviewing at NeXT. The accountant got so angry he nearly punched Jobs. But Jobs liked the accountant's no-nonsense attitude. He hired the man.

Jobs spent the next few years hard at work on software for his new company. The software was called NeXTstep. His cash poured into the company. Meanwhile, no products emerged. The first years were exciting, but difficult. Jobs felt depressed after leaving Apple. He complained that his fame was both a blessing and a curse. He often referred to "the other Steve," the public figure no one understood.[5]

Jobs sold $100 million worth of Apple stock to support NeXT. Unfortunately, he chose the wrong time to sell. He sold all but one share of stock in 1986. At that time the shares were worth less than $15. Jobs now had only a portion of his past fortune. Even so, he still had an eye for a good deal. In 1986, he purchased the Pixar animation studio from filmmaker George Lucas. Now he had two companies to manage.

After three years, many considered NeXT a failure. Jobs had wanted to produce computer hardware and software for education. His goal proved noble, but he ended up giving away more than he sold. By the end of 1988, business looked grim. The company should have produced 10,000 computers per month. Instead, it turned out only 400 per month. NeXT's computer, the Cube, cost $10,000. That proved too expensive for educators, and NeXT did not sell very many. In March 1989, Jobs decided to market the Cube through a store chain called Businessland. He hoped to move 10,000 Cubes by year's end. When 1989 ended, the store had sold only 360 machines.

Because NeXT was a private company, its lack of income was not public knowledge. Many still considered NeXT an innovative company. For a brief time, Jobs could have sold his company to his competitor, IBM. IBM had invested $60 million in NeXT. However, Jobs made it clear that he was not interested in letting IBM develop hardware for NeXT. He wanted to do that himself. Before long, IBM terminated the relationship.

For Jobs, 1989 could have ended miserably. But suddenly, his other company, Pixar, made news.

Toy Story *was such a success for Pixar that the movie's superhero,* Buzz Lightyear, *became the subject of an animated action-comedy* series, produced by Walt Disney Television Animation.

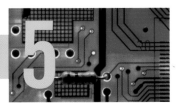

Back Again

I n 1989, the Pixar film *Tin Toy* won an Academy Award for Best Animated Short Film. The movie also won a prize for its computer-assisted animation. Pixar had not yet made a profit, but it showed promise.

Things were looking up for Steve Jobs. In 1991 he married Laurene Powell, whom he had dated since 1989. They had a son, Reed Paul, the following year. In May 1991, the Disney Corporation decided to invest in Pixar. Their money supported the company's new project, the movie *Toy Story*.

Good news from Pixar helped balance bad news from NeXT. Jobs had worked hard on NeXT's software. Still, the company was not profitable. NeXT shut down its hardware division in 1993.

But Jobs had two reasons to celebrate in 1995. His family grew with the birth of his third child, Erin Sienna. And after four long years of work, Pixar's first feature-length film, *Toy Story*, proved a triumph.

Meanwhile, Apple president John Sculley was having trouble making Apple succeed. The company had suffered since the departure of Woz and Jobs. The value of Apple stock had sunk to less than $10 per share. In 1996, John Sculley left Apple in disgrace. Later that year, Jobs received a call from the new Apple president, Gil Amelio. Amelio asked Jobs to return to Apple. Jobs agreed.

In the fall of 1996, Jobs became Apple's temporary CEO. Apple fans rejoiced. They felt sure Jobs would find a way to revive the company. Jobs did not disappoint them. He immediately promoted several new ideas to rescue Apple. At Macworld in 1997 he announced a new advertising campaign. He also said Apple would stop producing its less successful computers, such as the Newton. It would begin to work on new Mac designs.

Then Jobs stunned his audience with the biggest news of all. He announced that he was forming a partnership with his one-time enemy, Bill Gates of Microsoft. Microsoft had agreed to pay for the ideas it had borrowed from Apple to create its Windows program. And Apple had agreed to reconfigure its computers so they could run Windows software. Many people were put off by this plan. Apple lovers had held a low opinion of Microsoft for years. Now Jobs was asking them to accept the company as Apple's newest partner. But before long, the success of the partnership gained new fans for Apple.

In February 1997, Apple bought NeXT's software programs. Apple continued to develop the NeXT software for use with its Macs.

When Gil Amelio left Apple in July of 1997, Jobs gained complete control of his old company. He still liked to be dramatic, but now he performed in a positive way. At the January 6, 1998, Macworld meeting, he told the audience, "I almost forgot . . . We're profitable."[1] The audience shouted and cheered in reply. Soon Apple's stock would triple in value.

Jobs did not intend to rest and enjoy his success. In May 1998, Apple introduced a new version of the Macintosh, the iMac. It looked like no other computer. It had a translucent case that came in many bright colors. Its appealing software made it extremely popular. That same month, Jobs had a second reason to celebrate. He and Laurene welcomed another child, Eve.

Both Apple and Pixar continued to succeed. Pixar's next movie, *A Bug's Life,* premiered in November 1998. By the summer of 1999, it had surpassed *Toy Story's* earnings. Apple continued to produce innovative products like the PowerMac G3 and a portable computer called the ibook/SE. Apple redesigned its software so that it could be used by other personal computer users. IBM and other manufacturers returned the favor. This helped ensure Apple's survival. Apple also came out with a non-computer product called the iPod. The iPod was a small music player with a hard drive. It let users save lots of music to enjoy anytime they wanted.

In 2000, Steve Jobs became the permanent CEO of Apple. He drew a yearly salary of only $1.00. He did, however, collect large bonuses each year. His supporters knew that he deserved those bonuses. Jobs's leadership assured Apple's place in the competitive technology world.

Evidence of Apple's renewed importance could be seen at the 2001 Macworld Convention. The annual event had once featured only Apple products and services. In 2001, it offered exhibits by over 400 companies. They included competitors and one-time enemies such as IBM, Epson, Microsoft, and Hewlett-Packard.

At the 2002 Macworld, Jobs unveiled a newly designed iMac that was so unusual it made the cover

APPLE'S EARNINGS

YEAR	PROFIT OR LOSS
1997	Loss of $1.045 billion
1998	Profit of $309 million
1999	Profit of $601 million
2000	Profit of $786 million
2001	Loss of $25 million
2002	As of the first fiscal quarter of 2002, Apple posted a profit of $36 million

Soon after Steve Jobs returned to Apple, the company produced the first iMac desktop and laptop computers, which came with translucent cases. Available in an array of bright colors, the new computers proved that Apple was back on the cutting edge of computer design.

of *Time* magazine. Its small base looked like half a melon. A flat screen stood on top of a tube connecting it to the base. The tube allowed users to adjust the position of the screen. Reporters and Apple fans raved over the machine. As always, they could depend on Jobs to turn the computer world upside down.

When Jobs first returned to Apple, the company adopted a new slogan: "Think Different." The attitude that "different is good" represents Steve Jobs's approach to life. He has always viewed his future as a chance for change.

CHRONOLOGY

1955 Steve (Paulis) Jobs is born on February 24.

1972 Steve graduates from Homestead High School and attends classes at Reed College.

1974 Steve takes his first job as a video game designer for Atari, Inc.

1976 Steve founds Apple computer with Steve Wozniak.

1977 Apple introduces the Apple II Computer.

1978 Steve's daughter, Lisa, is born.

1980 Apple becomes a public company.

1983 Jobs asks John Sculley to become president of Apple.

1984 Jobs introduces the Macintosh computer.

1985 Jobs resigns from Apple and founds NeXT.

1986 Jobs buys Pixar, an animation studio.

1989 NeXT's first computer is a failure; Pixar's film *Tin Toy* wins an Academy Award.

1991 Jobs marries Laurene Powell on March 18.

1992 A son, Reed Paul is born.

1993 NeXT shuts down its hardware division.

1995 Jobs's third child, Erin Sienna is born; Pixar releases *Toy Story.*

1996 Steve Jobs returns to Apple.

1998 Apple introduces the iMac; Jobs's fourth child, Eve, is born; Pixar releases *A Bug's Life.*

2000 Pixar wins an Academy Award of Merit.

2001 Apple introduces the iBook notebook computer and the iPod music player.

2002 Apple releases a newly designed iMac at Macworld; Steve Jobs and the new iMac make the cover of *Time* magazine.

CHAPTER NOTES

CHAPTER ONE. Victory

1. Alan Deutschman, *The Second Coming of Steve Jobs* (New York: Broadway Books, 2000), p. 218.

CHAPTER TWO. A Young Man with a Vision

1. Jay Cocks, "The Updated Book of Jobs," *Time Magazine,* January 3, 1983, p. 26.
2. Ibid, p. 26.

CHAPTER THREE. Welcome to the World of Apple

1. Ann M. Morrison, "Apple Bites Back," *Fortune,* February 20, 1984, p. 86.
2. Linda M. Scott, "For the Rest of Us: A Reader-Oriented Interpretation of Apple's 1984 Commercial," *Journal of Popular Culture,* Summer, 1984, p. 72.

CHAPTER FOUR. NeXT

1. Eric Gelman and Michael Rogers, "Showdown in Silicon Valley," *Newsweek,* September 30, 1985, p. 46.
2. Jennet Conant and William D. Marbach, "It's the Apple of His Eye," *Newsweek,* January 30, 1984, p.56.
3. Gelman and Rogers, p. 47.
4. Ibid, p. 40.
5. Alan Deutschman, *The Second Coming of Steve Jobs* (New York: Broadway Books, 2000), p. 23.

CHAPTER FIVE. Back Again

1. Alan Deutschman, *The Second Coming of Steve Jobs* (New York: Broadway Books, 2000), p. 266.

GLOSSARY

Apple Computer Company—A computer company founded by Steve Jobs and Steve Wozniak in 1976 with the purpose of selling personal computers.

avar—An animation term for a computer tool that helps make an animated character move.

binary—Consisting of two things or parts. The binary numbering system consists of only two numbers: ones and zeroes.

bit—The smallest piece of information that a computer can handle.

byte—The building blocks of computer information, expressed as ones and zeroes. One byte is equal to eight bits.

CD-ROM—A term that stands for "Compact Disc Read-Only Memory," a format for storing data on CDs. The term may refer to the disk itself or to the disk drive used to read CD-ROMs.

CEO (chief executive officer)—The person responsible for everything a company does.

computer animation—Still computer images displayed in rapid sequence, giving the appearance of movement.

CPU (central processing unit)—A chip or chips that carry out basic instructions that operate a computer.

disk drive—The slot in a computer where floppy disks may be inserted and read by the CPU.

floppy disk—A portable square plastic disk that can store computer information.

graphics—Non-text figures, such as pictures, tables, etc.

graphic interface—Technology that allows computer users to click on symbols on the screen to tell the computer to perform tasks.

hardware—The physical components of a computer.

icon—A small image on the screen representing a program, instruction, or other object.

microprocessor—A name sometimes applied to the Central Processing Unit (CPU) of a personal computer, usually on one chip.

Microsoft—A computer company founded by Bill Gates and Paul Allen in 1975.

mouse—A device that allows a computer user to point to areas on the computer screen. The mouse first appeared on an Apple computer.

network—A series of connected computers.

operating system—The software that allows a computer to operate.

platform—A synonym for an operating system.

software—A series of instructions that tells the hardware how to perform tasks.

stocks—Shares of businesses that are sold to investors.

storyboard—Animation term for a hand drawn blueprint of a movie.

FURTHER READING

Brashares, Ann. Steve Jobs: *Think Different.* Brookfield, Connecticut: Millbrook, 2001.

Claybourne, Anna. *Computer Dictionary for Beginners.* London: Usborne, 2001.

Deutschman, Alan. *The Second Coming of Steve Jobs.* New York: Broadway Books, 2000.

Gaines, Ann Graham. *Steve Jobs.* Elkton, Maryland: Mitchell Lane, 2000.

Hjortberg, Charles A. *Kids and Computers.* Edina, Minnesota: Abdo & Daughters, 2000.

Kendall, Martha E. *Steve Wozniak: The Man Who Grew the Apple.* New York: Walker & Company, 1995.

Levy, Steven. *Insanely Great: The Life and Times of Macintosh, the Computer that Changed Everything.* New York: Viking, 1994.

Linzmeyer, Owen W. *Apple Confidential: The Real Story of Apple Computer.* San Francisco: No Starch Press, 1999.

Rozakis, Laurie. *Steven Jobs.* Vero Beach, Florida: Rourke Enterprises, Inc., 1993.

INTERNET ADDRESSES

Apple Computer's official Web site.
http://www.apple.com

The official Web site of the Pixar Company.
http://www.pixar.com

An online biography of Steve Jobs and a history of Apple Computer.
http://ei.cs.vt.edu/~history/Jobs.html

INDEX